Prayer Through Pictures: Helping Children of All Abilities Pray and Seek God

PRAYER THROUGH PICTURES

Helping Children of **All Abilities** Pray and Seek God

Danielle McManus
Illustrated by: Mara La Fratta Brennan & Brandon Watkins

NEW YORK

LONDON • NASHVILLE • MELBOURNE • VANCOUVER

Prayer Through Pictures

Helping Children of All Abilities Pray and Seek God

© 2025 Danielle McManus

Published in New York, New York, by Morgan James Publishing. Morgan James is a trademark of Morgan James, LLC. www.MorganJamesPublishing.com

Proudly distributed by Publishers Group West®

A **FREE** ebook edition is available for you
or a friend with the purchase of this print book.

CLEARLY SIGN YOUR NAME ABOVE

Instructions to claim your free ebook edition:
1. Visit MorganJamesBOGO.com
2. Sign your name CLEARLY in the space above
3. Complete the form and submit a photo
   of this entire page
4. You or your friend can download the ebook
   to your preferred device

ISBN 9781636985794 paperback
Library of Congress Control Number:

Cover Design and Interior Design by:
Alejandra Urquide

Morgan James is a proud partner of Habitat for Humanity Peninsula
and Greater Williamsburg. Partners in building since 2006.

Get involved today! Visit: www.morgan-james-publishing.com/giving-back

Dedication

This book is dedicated to my sons Jonah, Gavin, and Patrick, who helped shape me into the person God intended me to be.

Questions and answers for your child

What is prayer?
Prayer is how we talk to God. God is our father in heaven. He created us and watches over us from day-to-day. We can talk to God about anything. We can thank him for waking us up.

We can ask him to protect us when we leave our houses. We can ask him to help us do something. We can ask him to bless our families. God loves us just like our mom's and dad's do, so we should talk to him about everything all day long.

Why do we say certain things when we pray?
We usually start our prayers with God, Jesus, Heavenly Father, and words like that because we are addressing the person we are talking to. God has many names, so you can call him whatever you feel most comfortable with.

What does amen mean?
We end our prayers with amen. Amen means "so be it," which is a way of expressing that you want your prayer to agree with what God wants.

What does it mean to bless someone?
When we ask God to bless someone, that means we want God to look out for or watch over someone. Blessing someone can mean protecting them, helping them, comforting them, or being there for them in a way that only God can.

Content

It's Time to Pray

 Find a quiet place.

 Get on your knees.

 Place your hands together.

 Bow your head.

 Begin to talk with God.

Let's Pray Together

 Join hands.

 Bow your heads.

 Close your eyes.

 Quietly talk with God.

Prayers to Start
Your Day

In the morning, LORD, you hear my voice, in the morning I lay my requests before you and wait expectantly.
Psalm 5.3 (NIV)

Very early in the morning, while it was still dark, Jesus got up, left the house, and went off to a solitary place, where he prayed.
Mark 1:35 (NIV)

Jesus,

Thank you for waking me up this morning

and watching over me while I slept.

Please help me make good choices today

so you are happy with me, and your will is done.

Amen.

For I know the plans I have for you, declares the Lord, plans
to prosper you and not to harm you, plans to give you hope
and a future.
Jeremiah 29:11 (NIV)

Jesus,

Thank you for this day. Please help me

understand you better so that I can grow

into the person you want me to be.

Amen.

This is good, and pleases God our Savior, who wants all people to be saved and to come to a knowledge of the truth.
1 Timothy 2:3-4 (NIV)

God

Please be with me today. Help me to reach every goal

I have for myself and be the best person I can be.

I know that with you I am strong.

Amen.

> Have I not commanded you? Be strong and courageous. Do not be afraid; do not be discouraged, for the Lord your God will be with you wherever you go.
>
> Joshua 1:9 (NIV)

Jesus,

Today is another day that you have made, and I am glad.

  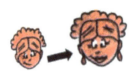

I will be the greatest person I can be today because

you said I am the head not the tail.

Amen.

> The Lord will make you the head, not the tail. If you pay attention to the commands of the Lord your God that I give you this day and carefully follow them, you will always be at the top, never at the bottom.
>
> Deuteronomy 28:13 (NIV)

Lord,

Be with me today as I go into the world. I will

listen to my teachers, complete my assignments,

and be kind to people. Thank you for never leaving me.

Amen.

For it is God's will that by doing good you should silence the ignorant talk of foolish people.
1 Peter 2:15(NIV)

Prayers for Meals

After he said this, he took some bread and gave thanks to God in front of them all. Then he broke it and began to eat.
Acts 27:35 (NIV)

Lord,

Thank you for this food. Please help me

take this meal and grow healthy and strong so that

I can do all the things you want me to do.

Amen.

Whoever regards one day as special does so to the Lord.
Whoever eats meat does so to the Lord, for they give thanks
to God; and whoever abstains does so to the Lord and gives
thanks to God.
Romans 14:6 (NIV).

Jesus,

Thank you God for giving us this food.

Thank you for knowing the things that we need

and providing us with enough to share.

Amen.

> **Then God said, "I give you every seed-bearing plant on the face of the whole earth and every tree that has fruit with seed in it. They will be yours for food."**
> Genesis 1:29 (NIV)

Lord,

Thank you for this food and the person that prepared it.

You always take care of us and make sure we are not

hungry or thirsty. With you, we will always have enough.

Amen.

Then Jesus declared, "I am the bread of life. Whoever comes to me will never go hungry, and whoever believes in me will never be thirsty."
John 6:35 (NIV)

God,

Thank you for all of the blessings you have given us.

Thank you for the clothes on our backs and the food

on this table. Thank you for providing for all of our needs.

Amen.

And he directed the people to sit down on the grass. Taking the five loaves and the two fish and looking up to heaven, he gave thanks and broke the loaves. Then he gave them to the disciples, and the disciples gave them to the people.
Matthew 14:19 (NIV)

Prayers at Night

By day the Lord directs his love, at night his song is with me—a prayer to the God of my life.

Psalm 42:8 (NIV)

One of those days Jesus went out to a mountainside to pray, and spent the night praying to God.

Luke 6:12 (NIV)

Jesus,

Thank you for watching over me today. Please forgive me

for any of my decisions today that made you sad. Help

   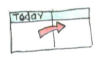

me make better choices tomorrow. I love you, Lord, and

thank you for loving me.

Amen.

> **Nothing in all creation is hidden from God's sight. Everything is uncovered and laid bare before the eyes of him to whom we must give account.**
> Hebrews 4:13 (NIV)

Lord,

     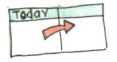

As I go to sleep tonight, I will not worry about tomorrow

because I know that you have a plan and I can count

on you to be with me. Please continue to watch over

me and my family. Goodnight, Lord.

Amen.

Cast all your anxiety on Him because he cares for you.
1 Peter 5:7

God,

Thank you for sending Jesus to help me. Today, some things

were good, and some things were bad, but I know you love

me. Please bless my family and friends and help everyone

to have a better day tomorrow.

Amen.

Bless those who curse you, pray for those who mistreat you.
Luke 6:28 (NIV)

Jesus,

Today I had a choice to make, but I didn't know what to do.

I know that you love me, and I need you to help me make

the right decision. Thank you for today and the choices I will

make tomorrow. Goodnight, Jesus.

Amen.

> **Trust in the Lord with all your heart and lean not on your own understanding.**
> Proverbs 3:5 (NIV)

The Lord's Prayer

Our Father which art in heaven, Hallowed be thy name.

Thy kingdom come, Thy will be done in earth, as it is in

heaven. Give us this day our daily bread. And forgive us

our debts, as we forgive our debtors. And lead us not

into temptation, but deliver us from evil: For thine is the

kingdom, and the power, and the glory, forever.

Matthew 6:9-13 (KJV)   **Amen.**

Everywhere you go, and in everything you do, remember,

He loves you.

About the author

As a veteran early childhood special education teacher, small business owner, and mother of two children diagnosed with autism, Danielle McManus understands the highs and lows that many parents of young children go through. As a Christian, she longed to share the beauty and relationship she found in God with her children but struggled to know how. She did not want to just teach her children words, she wanted them to understand what those words meant, and equip them with the knowledge and understanding to eventually seek God on their own. Prayer Through Pictures was formed through that desire.

Born in Richmond, VA, Danielle holds a bachelor's degree in psychology from Virginia Commonwealth University, a master's degree in early childhood unified education from the University of Kansas, and a master's certificate in Educational Leadership from the University of Kansas. Danielle has spent her life devoted to helping children and adults with disabilities. She has worked as a caregiver for individuals with disabilities, a special education teacher, a professional mentor and instructional coach, a master trainer for churches and organizations wanting to increase their knowledge and understanding of children with disabilities and their families. She remains a proud wife and mother to her amazing family.

www.ingramcontent.com/pod-product-compliance
Lightning Source LLC
Jackson TN
JSHW071008120625
85971JS00021B/600